Contents

Words in **bold** are in the glossary.

The piano

A piano is a musical instrument. You sit down and use both hands to play it.

Pianos usually have eighty-eight **keys**. Some of these are white and some are black.

The case of a piano is made of wood. The keys in modern pianos are made of wood and plastic.

This girl is playing a piano.

Let's Make
MUSIC

The Piano
and other keyboard instruments

Rita Storey

FRANKLIN WATTS
LONDON·SYDNEY

First published in 2007 by
Franklin Watts
338 Euston Road
London NW1 3BH

Franklin Watts Australia
Level 17/207 Kent Street
Sydney NSW 2000

Art director: Jonathan Hair
Series designed and created for Franklin Watts by Painted Fish Ltd.
Designer: Rita Storey
Editor: Fiona Corbridge
Adviser: Helen MacGregor

Picture credits
istockphoto.com pp. 4, 5, 7, 12, 16, 17, 20, 21, 22, 23, 24, 25; Robin Little/Redferns
p. 26; Tudor Photography pp. 3, 6, 8, 9, 10, 11, 13, 14, 18, 19;
Ulster Orchestra p. 15.

Cover images: Tudor Photography, Banbury (top); istock.com (bottom left,
middle and right)

All photos posed by models.
Thanks to Husnen Ahmad, Hannah Barton and Maddi Indun

ISBN 978 0 7496 7582 0

A CIP catalogue record for this book is available from the British Library.
Dewey classification: 786

Printed in China

Frankin Watts is a division of Hachette Children's Books,
an Hachette Livre UK company.

Making a sound

To make a sound on a piano, press the keys with your fingers.

Different sounds

Each key makes a different sound, or musical note. You can press them one by one or several together.

Listen!
Page 28 tells you about music played on keyboard instruments that you can listen to.

Keys

The sound

When you press a piano key, it makes a tiny hammer hit a metal string inside the piano. The string begins to wobble very fast – it is vibrating.

Sound waves

When the string **vibrates**, it makes the air around it move as well. The way that the air moves is called a **sound wave**.

Louder

The sound waves bounce around inside the piano and make the sounds louder.

Pressing the keys moves the hammers inside a piano.

8

Stopping the sound

When you take your fingers off the keys, pads stop the strings vibrating. These pads are called dampers.

Tuning

To make each string play the correct note, a piano has to be tuned. This is done by turning the tuning pegs.

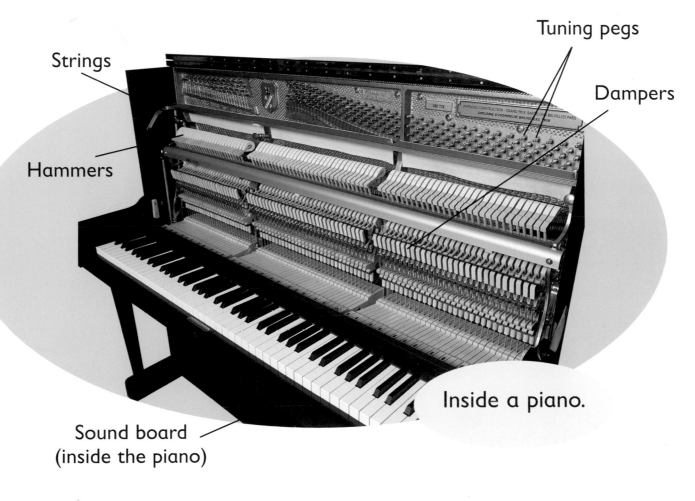

Strings

Tuning pegs

Dampers

Hammers

Inside a piano.

Sound board
(inside the piano)

The keys

Each key on a piano makes a different sound. You can press several keys together to make lots of different sounds.

High and low

Some musical notes are high and some are low. We call this their **pitch**.

Keys that play notes with the lowest pitch

A piano keyboard.

Keys that play notes with the highest pitch

Keyboard

The line of keys on a piano is called a keyboard. The sound that each key plays goes from high pitch at one end of the keyboard to low pitch at the other end.

Playing notes

To make quiet sounds, press the keys gently. For loud sounds, press them hard.

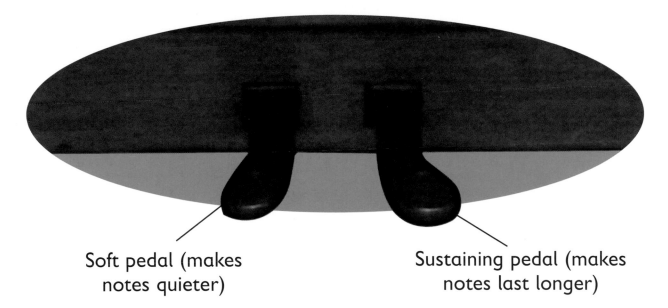

Soft pedal (makes notes quieter)

Sustaining pedal (makes notes last longer)

Pedals

There are two (or sometimes three) pedals near the floor, which you press with your feet. The one on the left makes the notes sound quieter, and the one on the right makes them last longer and seem louder.

Chords and scales

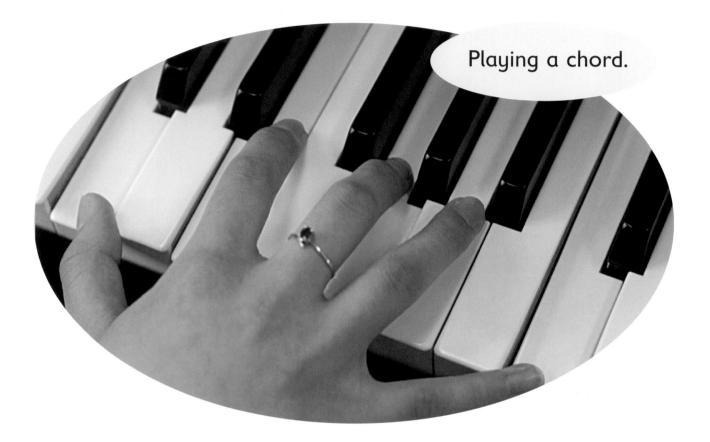

Playing a chord.

There are lots of different ways to play notes on a piano. A good pianist (piano player) uses both hands and plays up to ten keys at a time.

A chord

When two or more keys are held down together, the notes that are played are called a chord.

Black and white

The white keys on a piano keyboard play notes called **natural notes**. The black keys are grouped in twos and threes. They play notes called **sharps** and **flats**.

These keys play sharps and flats

Music notes

To be able to play music that other people have made up, or composed, you need to understand how to read music. Music is written in musical notes.

The notes are written on five lines called a stave. The place of a note on the stave tells us how high or low it is. This is called its pitch.

Notes are named after letters: A, B, C, D, E, F, G. **Symbols** tell us how long or short a note is. The length of the notes in a piece of music make up its **rhythm**.

A scale is a set of notes played up and then down the keyboard.
A scale of eight notes is called an octave. The octave shown here goes from one C on the keyboard to the next C. The notes are natural notes.

C D E F G A B C

C
D
E
F
G
A
B
C

These keys play natural notes

Upright or grand?

There are two kinds of piano – an upright piano and a grand piano.

Upright pianos

Most people who have a piano have an upright piano. It is sometimes called an acoustic piano.

An upright or acoustic piano.

A grand piano being played in an orchestra.

Grand pianos

Grand pianos are used in **orchestras** and played by pianists giving a **concert**.

The strings in a grand piano are laid flat, going away from the keyboard. A grand piano is larger than an upright piano but has the same number of keys.

There is a smaller type of grand piano called a baby grand.

Playing together

There are lots of different ways that a piano can be used.

Play along
The piano is often played to **accompany** singers and other **solo** instruments.

Singers may use a piano to help them sing notes at the correct pitch when they are practising or performing.

This pianist is accompanying a violinist as she practises.

Duets

Sometimes two people play a piano together. This is called a duet.

These performers are playing a duet.

Trios and quartets

A piano may be played with a small group of other instruments. A piano trio has a piano, a violin and a cello.

In a piano quartet, there are four instruments – a piano, a violin, a viola and a cello.

Electronic keyboard

On an electronic keyboard, you play the keys in the same way as on a piano. The keyboard must be plugged into the electricity supply to make it work.

When you press a key, the sound is produced **electronically**.

Playing an electronic keyboard.

Rhythms

The keyboard can play different rhythms and beats in the background as you play the keys. It can also be made to sound like other instruments.

Light keyboards

Keyboards that you use at home or at school usually have fewer than eighty-eight keys. They are easy to carry from place to place.

The controls on an electronic keyboard.

19

Computer music

This girl is playing a midi keyboard attached to a computer.

Many electronic keyboards can be linked to a computer.

Midi keyboard

A midi keyboard does not produce a sound when you play it. It sends a signal to a computer, which changes it into music.

The sounds are passed through **amplifiers** and **loudspeakers** so that they can be heard.

New sounds

The computer can use the signals from the keyboard to do other things. It can change sounds that have been stored in the computer, or produce new sounds.

It can also copy the sound of all sorts of musical instruments.

Music notes

A person who writes new pieces of music is called a composer.

When composers are making up music, they often play the notes on a keyboard. If they use a keyboard connected to a computer, they can change the notes to make lots of different sounds.

These controls can change the sounds.

Pipe organ

A pipe organ is a wind instrument. It makes sounds by blowing air through pipes of different sizes.

Playing a pipe organ

There are at least two keyboards, which you play with your hands. There are also lots of pedals that you play with your feet.

Organ stops

The sound of the pipes can be changed by pulling controls called organ stops.

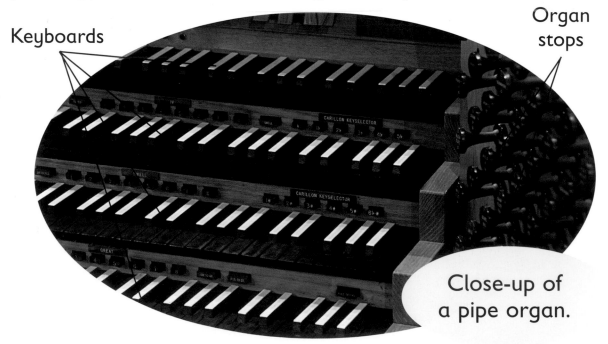

Keyboards

Organ stops

Close-up of a pipe organ.

Pipes

Bellows blow air through the organ pipes, which are different sizes. The large pipes make a deep, low sound. The small pipes make a high-pitched sound.

A big sound

Pipe organs are very large and are often used in buildings such as churches, because they make a loud sound.

Organ pipes in a church.

Other keyboards

Other musical instruments also have a keyboard that you play.

Harpsichord

The harpsichord looks a bit like a piano, but it sounds very different. When the player presses the keys on the keyboard, small hooks called quills pluck the strings.

Harmonium
The harmonium is a type of organ. It is often used to play Indian music.

Electric organ

An electric organ is smaller than a pipe organ and does not have pipes.

Accordion

The accordion is played by using a keyboard and a set of buttons. You have to squeeze a set of bellows in and out as you play, and the air from this makes the sound.

Key notes

Keyboard instruments can be used to play many different styles of music.

Jazz

Jazz is a style of music that began in New Orleans, USA. The sound of the piano is an important part of jazz music.

Pop and rock

Pop and rock musicians use electronic keyboards and computers to make strange and exciting sounds.

This band is making music using electronic keyboards.

Listen!

Websites

Listen to all the notes of a piano (played from low to high), hear special effects, and discover other keyboard instruments such as the celeste and synthesizer, with the BBC Radio 3 Guide to the Orchestra at: *www.bbc.co.uk/orchestras/guide*

Play tunes on a virtual piano and learn the names of the notes; choose a chord or scale and you will see and hear the notes so that you can practise them yourself. Go to: *www.primaryresources.co.uk/music/piano.html*

Play your favourite tunes, to a backing of drumbeats, on a virtual keyboard. Explore the sounds you can make by selecting an instrument, drum pattern or chord mode and clicking on the 'piano' keys to listen to the sounds. Go to: *www.bgfl.org/bgfl/custom/resources_ftp/client_ftp/ks2/music/piano/index.htm*

Watch a video about a young classical pianist and hear her play with the Guildford Symphony Orchestra at: *www.bbc.co.uk/southerncounties/content/articles/2007/02/27/forty_eight_young_musician_feature.shtml*

At 'A Young Person's Guide to the Organ' you can listen to pieces of organ music as you read about the history of the pipe organ. You can see a plan of the parts of an organ and listen to samples of different pipes. Go to: *www.agohq.org/guide/*

Listen to many different pieces played on the accordion at:
www.accordion-online.de/e_mp3.htm

CDs

Piano
Mozart: *Variations on 'Ah, vous dirai-je, Maman'* ('Twinkle, Twinkle, Little Star').
Beethoven: *Für Elise*; Piano Sonatas.
Saint-Saëns: *Carnival of the Animals*.
Scott Joplin: *Piano Rags*.
Dave Brubeck: *Take Five*.
Sparky's Magic Piano.
Schumann: *Scenes of Childhood*.
Chopin: Mazurkas and Waltzes.
Debussy: *Children's Corner*.
Percy Grainger: *English Country Garden*.
Eric Satie: *Gymnopedies*.
Duke Ellington: *C Jam Blues*.
Steve Reich: *Six Pianos*.

Organ
Bach: Preludes and Fugues.
Saint-Saëns: *Symphony No. 3 for Organ and Orchestra*.

Harpsichord
Scarlatti: Sonatas.
The Fitzwilliam Virginal Book.

Accordion
French Café Accordion Music.
Histoire du Tango.

Glossary

Accompany To play an instrument to support a singer or musician as he or she performs.

Amplifier Equipment for increasing the strength of a sound.

Bellows A device for making a strong flow of air.

Concert A public musical performance by singers or musicians.

Electronic, electronically Using an electric system to produce or change a sound.

Flat A musical note that is pitched slightly lower than the natural note of the same letter (e.g. G flat is lower than G).

Key A lever on an instrument that you press down to play.

Loudspeaker A device for changing electrical signals into sounds that we can hear.

Natural notes Notes played by the white keys on a piano.

Orchestra A large group of performers playing various musical instruments.

Pitch A high musical note or sound is said to have a high pitch. A low musical note or sound is said to have a low pitch.

Rhythm The regular pattern of sound in music.

Sharp A musical note that is pitched slightly higher than the natural note of the same letter (e.g. G sharp is higher than G).

Solo Playing alone.

Sound wave A wave that transmits sound through the air.

Symbol A shape used to represent something else.

Vibrating; vibrates; vibration Moving backwards and forwards, or up and down, quickly; this movement.

29

Index